TERRORIST ATTACKS

THE ATTACK ON U.S. MARINES IN LEBANON ON OCTOBER 23, 1983

Steven P. Olson

The Rosen Publishing Group, Inc.
New York

To the 241 soldiers, gone but not forgotten

Published in 2003 by The Rosen Publishing Group, Inc.
29 East 21st Street, New York, NY 10010

Copyright © 2003 by The Rosen Publishing Group, Inc.

First Edition

All rights reserved. No part of this book may be reproduced in any form without permission in writing from the publisher, except by a reviewer.

Library of Congress Cataloging-in-Publication Data
Olson, Steven P.
The attack on U.S. Marines in Lebanon on October 23, 1983/by Steven P. Olson.—1st ed.
    p. cm.—(Terrorist attacks)
Includes bibliographical references and index.
Contents: "The Paris of the Mediterranean"—Israel and the PLO—Israel invades Lebanon—Here come the marines—Spring and summer 1983—The aftermath.
ISBN 978-1-4358-9084-8
1. United States Marine Compound Bombing, Beirut, Lebanon, 1983.
2. United States—Foreign relations—Lebanon. 3. Lebanon—Foreign relations—United States. 4. Lebanon—History—Israeli intervention, 1982-1984. 5. United Nations—Peace-keeping forces—Lebanon.
6. United States. Marine Corps—History—Arab-Israeli conflict. [1. United States Marine Compound Bombing, Beirut, Lebanon, 1983. 2. Terrorism. 3. Bombings.]
I. Title. II. Series.
DS87.53.O47 2002
956.05'2—dc21

2002010754

Manufactured in the United States of America

CONTENTS

	Introduction	4
Chapter 1	"The Paris of the Mediterranean"	9
Chapter 2	Israel and the PLO	17
Chapter 3	Israel Invades Lebanon	27
Chapter 4	Here Come the Marines	35
Chapter 5	Spring and Summer 1983	41
Chapter 6	The Aftermath	51
	Glossary	58
	For More Information	59
	For Further Reading	61
	Bibliography	62
	Index	63

INTRODUCTION

At about 6:20 AM on October 23, 1983, a yellow five-ton truck stopped at the north checkpoint outside of Beirut International Airport at Khalde, Lebanon. The Lebanese guards who worked at the checkpoint that morning did not notice that the bed of the Mercedes-Benz truck was pushed lower than it should have been. The truck was carrying a heavy load.

Perhaps the hazy morning sun coming over the Chouf Mountains above East Beirut made it difficult for the guards to see. The city of Beirut sits inside a bowl formed by the mountains to the east and the ocean to the north and west. In this bowl, there was often a cloud of smog from the activities of the busy city. Adding to the smog may have been a dull layer of smoke from the fighting that was a daily part of Beirut life. In the city and the mountains to the east, seventeen different militias were in the middle of an eight-year-old civil war.

Behind the checkpoint, several hundred U.S. Marines were asleep in their barracks. Although the marines were in Beirut as part of an international peacekeeping

A Middle East Airlines jet prepares for takeoff from Beirut's Khalde International Airport, just west of the site where the U.S. Marines base was bombed.

force, many of these militias, who have a long-standing hatred for the U.S. government, saw them as Americans first. For months, artillery shells and missiles had pounded marine positions inside the airport and along its perimeter. From the bombed-out apartments across the street from the airport, snipers had shot at marines walking to the mess hall, filling sandbags, or cleaning their gear. While their training told the marines to take the high ground in the mountains above them, leaders in the U.S. government had ordered them to stay at the airport, occasionally allowing them to return fire.

The Attack on U.S. Marines in Lebanon on October 23, 1983

It had been quiet for the previous two days, however, and peace and quiet in Beirut was what the marines wanted. At 6:20 AM, most of the marines were asleep in the Battalion Landing Team (BLT) headquarters at the Marine Amphibious Unit (MAU) compound.

Like so many that had passed through the gates in the fourteen months since the marines had landed at the Beirut airport, the loaded Mercedes truck was waved through. It proceeded southward at a steady pace along the airport road. To the driver's right, beyond the airport runway, lay the beautiful Mediterranean Sea. To his left ran an iron fence that separated the road from the marines' compound.

Just south of the marines' compound sat the airport terminal, a symbol that the city of Beirut was still connected to the outside world. The driver turned left in front of the airport terminal and pulled into the empty parking lot. Later, some argued that the parking lot should have been fortified with mines and trenches. However, people using the airport needed someplace to park. The parking lot was free of mines, free of sandbags, and free of trenches.

The driver of the truck drove in circles around the parking lot, gathering speed. He turned his fast and heavy truck and headed north, crossing out of the parking lot. Marines at two sentry posts were shocked to see the truck barrel through a thick roll of razor wire that was stretched

Introduction

across the south end of the marines' compound. Immediately, they began firing at the truck.

The driver continued to accelerate as he and his truck sped past the two guard shacks, the mess tents, and the showers. One unarmed marine saw the passing truck and a smile on the driver's face. Traveling at least fifty miles per hour, the driver and his truck jumped the single step leading to the BLT building and crashed through the front door.

Twelve thousand pounds of dynamite detonated among the sleeping marines. The four-story building collapsed to eye level, and many who were not lucky enough to die instantly were buried under tons of rubble. From a few miles away, some witnesses saw such a large cloud over the airport that they believed a nuclear weapon had been detonated. To others even farther away, it sounded like another round of artillery on another morning in war-torn Beirut.

As U.S. Marines and Lebanese rescue workers rushed to the collapsed BLT building, as bodies were pulled from the rubble, as snipers took shots at the rescuers, the questions began to form. But two loomed like clouds over the United States and its military: Who was the driver? And why did he do it?

This book explores the complex answers to these two simple questions.

A building is bombed in Bhamdoun, Lebanon, during Lebanon's civil war.

"The Paris of the Mediterranean"

CHAPTER 1

An enormous amount of war and suffering has been packed into the tiny nation of Lebanon. Located north of Israel on the coast of the Mediterranean Sea, Lebanon is 135 miles long and 50 miles wide with a ridge of mountains running north–south through the middle of the country. Dappled with olive orchards that flourish in the warm, dry climate, this tiny country is home to at least fifteen different religious, political, and military groups who are willing to kill each other or die trying to do so.

South of Lebanon is Israel, the nation that occupies lands sacred to three major religions: Judaism,

The Attack on U.S. Marines in Lebanon on October 23, 1983

Christianity, and Islam. Jews, Christians, and Muslims have fought each other for centuries for control of these lands, and the fighting has often spilled over into lands that include the modern nation of Lebanon.

Over many centuries and many wars, these three great religions have splintered into many groups. In the Middle East, Sunnis, Shiites, Druze, and Palestinians may all call themselves Muslims. Although they share many religious beliefs, they are deeply divided on other issues. For example, in the seventh century, the grandson of Muhammad, the founder of Islam, was killed by people who opposed his leadership of the Muslims. These people, who believed in elected leadership of the Muslim faith, became Sunnis, while those who followed the descendants of Muhammad and his grandson became Shiites. The wars between Sunnis and Shiites have splintered nations and created new factions across the Middle East and Asia.

The Druze and Maronites

To Lebanon, some of these splinter groups, like the Shiites, are new arrivals, and some, like the Druze, have been living in the shadow of Mount Lebanon for a thousand years.

The Druze faith began in Egypt sometime in the tenth century, and its people wandered through the Middle East until they settled in the hills of southeast Lebanon. There, the Druze prospered and expanded into the Chouf Mountains, yet they remained closed to outsiders. Today, to call oneself Druze is to

A member of the Progressive Socialist Party (PSP), a Druze faction, sets up a roadblock in Beirut with a picture of PSP leader Walid Joumblatt.

be able to trace one's ancestors back to the people who first settled in Lebanon a thousand years ago.

Founded by a Christian priest, John Maron, in the fifth century, the Maronites, like the Druze, escaped persecution and settled on the slopes of Mount Lebanon. When Syria was conquered by Muslims in the seventh century, the Maronite people fled into the mountains in Lebanon, where they gained their freedom of religion and their identity as a group.

Over the years, the Maronites created links with Christian nations such as France. They discovered that silk and olives from their orchards on Mount Lebanon were of great value in the West. Their connections with traders to the east of

The Attack on U.S. Marines in Lebanon on October 23, 1983

Lebanon made them perfect middlemen to bridge the distance between the wealth of the West and the goods of the East.

Beirut became the center of this trading and prosperity. People of many religions and nations found common ground in the markets and shops in the streets of Beirut, and the common language was money. Over time, these various cultures changed the face of this unique city, until it became known as the Paris of the Mediterranean.

The Beginnings of Conflict

As the Middle East became dominated by Muslim groups, the prospering Maronites found themselves in conflict with their neighbors. Thanks to their trade with Christian nations, the Maronites had become wealthy landholders and had begun to spread southward into the holy lands of the Druze. Open warfare between the Druze and the Maronites began in 1860. The ensuing fighting was fierce and often horrible. It is believed that thousands of Christian Maronites were massacred on the slopes of the Chouf Mountains.

To the rescue of the Maronites came France, which remained in Lebanon to protect its trade in the Middle East. Under the protection of the French, the Maronites continued to rise. They became richer, more powerful, and greater in numbers.

World War II, however, changed the face of Lebanon forever. The fall of France to Germany in 1940 weakened its

Nebi Shueib is a holy site for the Druze people of Lebanon.

influence in Lebanon. In 1943, Lebanon was granted its independence from France. Power in the new nation was divided between the competing groups in a document known as the National Pact. A 1932 population census in Lebanon indicated that Maronite Christians were the largest group, so the National Pact reserved the presidency for the Maronites and the lesser office of the prime minister for Sunni Muslims. The Druze, the Shiites, and other groups were left out. This was a mistake.

The Druze Found the PSP

When the National Pact left the Druze out of political power in Lebanon, they formed their own political party. The Progressive

The Attack on U.S. Marines in Lebanon on October 23, 1983

Socialist Party (PSP) was founded in May 1949 by Kamal Joumblatt. Among other goals, the PSP charter supported government ownership of Lebanon's industries and resources, which at the time were mostly controlled by the Maronite Christians. Also, the PSP supported the cause of the Palestinian people to regain their homes from Israel.

Over time, Joumblatt expanded the PSP and gathered more power for the Druze people until he was assassinated by unknowns on March 16, 1977. Control of the PSP passed to his son, Walid, and fighting between Druze and Christians continued.

The Green Line

Maronites, Sunnis, Druze, and Shiites all contributed to the unrest in Lebanon. There were conflicts between religions. There were conflicts over control of valuable trade. There were conflicts over politics.

Despite these struggles, Beirut remained a thriving city of trade and culture throughout the 1950s and 1960s. Museums, cafés, music clubs, and restaurants allowed Christians, Jews, and Muslims of many cultures to mix in the narrow streets. Whether its soldiers were involved in the violence or not, each group brought its culture, cuisine, language, and values to Beirut.

By 1983, the older people of Beirut spoke of the 1950s and 1960s with a great nostalgia. In place of the Paris of the Mediterranean lay a deeply scarred city divided in

In March 1965, people of many cultures danced and listened to music together in Beirut's "Acapulco Beach" area. After the Lebanese civil war began in 1975, the relaxed, worldly atmosphere of Beirut became a memory.

two. Named for the green grass and shrubs that grew around destroyed buildings and in cracks in the streets, the Green Line separated Christian East Beirut from Muslim West Beirut. To cross the line was to risk one's life, for the bullet-ridden buildings that lined the wide streets of the Green Line and the rubble of Martyr's Square were occupied by snipers who shot at anyone. They shot because that was what they knew. They knew to shoot because that was what they had seen in the streets of Beirut since 1975, when the Lebanese civil war took the first of the 50,000 lives that would be lost over the next fifteen years.

East Jerusalem, a Muslim district, with the Dome of the Rock in the foreground

ISRAEL AND THE PLO

CHAPTER 2

As Lebanon gained independence from France and began to slide toward civil war, the nation of Israel to the south also gained its independence, pushed its borders outward, and began to develop. These neighboring countries, headed in opposite directions, would later collide in the streets of downtown Beirut.

History of Israel

The history of the nation of Israel began in the sixth century BC, when Palestine, the land centered on the city of Jerusalem, was overrun by the Babylonians, and the Jewish people living there were marched

This engraving by Gustave Doré depicts the people of Jerusalem mourning the loss of their city to the Babylonians after a sixteen-month siege, circa 586 BC.

Israel and the PLO

to Babylon. Their prophets told them that one day they would return to Palestine. This was not to be for a long time.

Over the centuries, the Jewish people spread out across many nations in the Middle East and Europe, where they were often persecuted. The Diaspora, the spreading of the Jewish people to lands outside of Palestine, continued for more than twenty centuries. A large number of Jews eventually settled in the United States.

Yet, there was always hope among them of returning to Palestine. In 1896, a Hungarian writer named Theodore Herzl published *The Jewish State*, a book that outlined the sources of anti-Jewish feelings and suggested that the best solution was to create a Jewish nation. Thus, Zionism, the movement to create a Jewish nation, was born.

At the end of World War I, Britain wanted to take control of the lands of Palestine from the Ottoman Empire and sought Jewish cooperation to secure it. In return for political help from international Jewish groups to support British control of Palestine, Britain declared its approval for the establishment of a national home for the Jewish people in Palestine at some future date. When Britain did gain control of Palestine, there was much rejoicing by Jews all over the world. Carrying hope in their hearts, Jews began to move back to Palestine. This return to Palestine caused problems with the Arabs already living there.

By 1939, the Arab population in Palestine was in full rebellion against the British and against the Jewish immigrants.

The Attack on U.S. Marines in Lebanon on October 23, 1983

To make peace with the Arabs, Britain promised the formation of an Arab nation in Palestine, as well. The British had promised a country in the same holy lands to both the Arabs and the Jews.

During World War II, the Nazis tried to destroy the Jews living in Europe. Over six million Jews were executed by the Nazis in the streets of Germany, in the gas chambers of eastern Europe, and on the battlefields of the war. This persecution and the threat to the Jewish race strengthened the Zionists' commitment to creating a homeland for Jews.

After the massacre of Jews in World War II, the Zionist movement gained support from nations such as the United States. On November 29, 1947, the United Nations resolved to form two nations, one Arab and one Jewish, in the lands of Palestine. This decision was called Resolution 181. Arabs rejected the plan.

On May 14, 1948, the British gave up control over Palestine. Immediately, the nation of Israel was formed. Palestinian Arabs were expelled from their homes by the more organized Jews. Thousands of Palestinians began their own diaspora.

In its first years, Israel struggled to secure its borders against the angry Arab populations that had been pushed aside. At the time Israel was mostly an agricultural economy and depended heavily on foreign aid, a large part of which came from the United States. If the United States had not assisted Israel in the first twenty years of its

Israel and the PLO

history, the nation of Israel might have been eliminated. To many Arabs today, the existence of the state of Israel is the fault of the United States. To them, both countries are equal enemies.

The Founding of the PLO

The Arabs expelled from Palestine were organized in loose groups in Egypt, Jordan, Syria, and other countries. In Jerusalem in 1964, these groups were united under one federation, called the Palestine Liberation Organization (PLO). In its charter, the PLO sought to organize the Palestinian people and to replace the nation of Israel. The PLO set up camp in Jordan, across the Jordan River from Palestine, and began to gather support from other Arab nations. At the same time, the PLO began terrorist operations across the river into Israel.

In 1967, Israel surprised its Arab neighbors by taking territory on its borders. In what became known as the Six-Day War, Israel took the Gaza Strip from Egypt, the Golan Heights from Syria, the West Bank from Jordan, and East Jerusalem from the Muslim world over the course of six days.

Angered by the capture of holy lands and monuments by the Jews, Arabs around the world gave more support to the PLO groups. One of the largest and most successful of the groups was Fatah, whose leader, Yasser Arafat, was elected chairman of the PLO in 1969.

The Attack on U.S. Marines in Lebanon on October 23, 1983

MIDDLE EAST GROUPS AT A GLANCE

Amal — The political party that represents a large Shiite Muslim faction in the slums of southern Beirut. The civil war and Israel's invasion forced Shiites out of their farms in southern Lebanon and created a lot of anger among them.

Druze — An offshoot of an offshoot of the Muslim faith. Druze trace their roots back to the original founders in the eleventh century. The Druze had been sharing and fighting over Mount Lebanon with the Maronites since 1860. Their political party is the Progressive Socialist Party (PSP).

Hezbollah — Hezbollah was founded by Shiite clerics in the southern slums of Beirut in 1982. Inspired by the Iranian Revolution in 1979, Hezbollah aimed to overthrow the Lebanese government and to replace it with a Shiite government.

Islam — One of the great religions of the Middle East, Islam was founded by the prophet Muhammad in 622 AD in the city of Medina, which is now in Saudi Arabia. Islam's followers are called Muslims and have since split into two main factions: Sunni and Shiite.

Islamic Jihad — Founded in Egypt in 1979, Islamic Jihad seeks to remove Israel and the United States from the Middle East. Islamic Jihad claimed responsibility for the attack on the U.S. Embassy in West Beirut in April 1983.

Israel and the PLO

Judaism — The religion of the Jews, among the first-known inhabitants of the area now called Israel. In the early part of the twentieth century, the Jews founded a movement called Zionism to create a homeland for their people. This homeland came into being in 1948 as the nation of Israel.

Lebanese Armed Forces — A coalition of Maronite Christian militias, the Lebanese Armed Forces (LAF) were used to protect Maronites before other groups. The U.S. government saw the LAF as the military of Lebanon, but many Lebanese felt they served only Christian interests.

Maronite Christians — The Maronite Christians have lived on the slopes of Mount Lebanon for centuries. The Maronites had been sharing and fighting over Mount Lebanon with the Druze since 1860. Their political party is the Phalange party, which has governed Lebanon since independence in 1943.

PLO — Short for Palestine Liberation Organization, the PLO is the political party of the Palestinian people who lost their homes when the nation of Israel was formed. Spread all across the Middle East, the PLO had many families and fighters living in Lebanon. In Israel and other countries, the PLO is considered a terrorist organization.

Yasser Arafat, leader of the PLO, during a 1980 interview with a Beirut magazine

Unified and financed, the PLO continued raids from the camps in Jordan against Israel, which responded severely against the PLO and its host, the nation of Jordan. Finally, in 1970, King Hussein of Jordan had had enough of the PLO and cracked down on the organization. About 10,000 Palestinians were killed in the fighting, and the PLO was kicked out of Jordan.

The PLO and the Lebanese Civil War

Fleeing Jordan, Arafat relocated the headquarters of the PLO to West Beirut. To the mix of Maronites, Druze, Sunnis, and Shiites was added the PLO, a heavily armed militia that was determined to bring down the nation of Israel at any cost.

In a few years, the PLO gained control of West Beirut and came into direct conflict with the ruling Maronites and their political party, the Phalange. On April 13, 1975, a bus carrying Palestinians was ambushed as it passed through a Christian suburb of East Beirut. All passengers were killed.

Thus began the Lebanese civil war. In the beginning, this struggle pitted the ruling Phalangists against the PLO and its allies among the Lebanese Muslims, like the Druze, who had been left out of Lebanese politics. The civil war soon enveloped all of the militias in Lebanon and trapped the nations of France, the United States, and Israel in a flame of war that would take 50,000 lives over a span of fifteen years.

An apartment complex comes under rocket fire during the Lebanese civil war. The fighting between PLO and Phalangist troops caused mass destruction in Beirut.

A patrol of the highly organized right-wing Phalangist militia marches through the Lebanese town of Zgharta.

Israel Invades Lebanon

CHAPTER 3

By 1976, the PLO had control of West Beirut, and the ruling Phalangists had a full civil war on their hands. The Christian Phalangists were bitterly opposed by the PLO and the Druze people. The PLO was a serious problem for the Phalangists, as it was for their neighbor to the south, Israel.

The Phalangists and Israel

The PLO had positioned artillery guns and even tanks in southern Lebanon. Artillery shells were falling on towns, farms, and villages in northern Israel, terrorizing the Israeli population.

Since 1976, Israel and the Maronite Christians had been talking

The Attack on U.S. Marines in Lebanon on October 23, 1983

in secret about the PLO, their common problem. To stay in control of their country during the civil war, the Phalangists needed weapons that they did not have. Israel had those weapons. By the end of 1976, weapons were flowing from Israel to the Phalangists. But it was not enough.

The Phalangists wanted Israel to come into Lebanon and clean out the PLO. However, their discussions were slow and difficult for the following reasons:

- If the Phalangists publicly invited the Israelis, who were Jews, into Lebanon, all the Muslim groups of Lebanon would then oppose the Phalangists. By 1976, Muslims outnumbered Christians in Lebanon.
- If the Phalangists invited the Israelis, they would anger Syria, their neighbor to the east. In 1976, Syria invaded Lebanon to help the Phalangists and had remained in Beirut and eastern Lebanon. An invasion by Israel, Syria's enemy, might spark a war between them on Lebanon's soil.
- If Israel invaded Lebanon, it had to quickly clean out the PLO and get out, for Israel had no interest in getting involved in Lebanon's internal problems. Israel had enough problems maintaining its borders.
- If Israel invaded Lebanon without invitation, Israel would anger the other nations in the Middle East and their greatest ally, the United States, which supplied most of their weapons.

Israel Invades Lebanon

Israel, the United States, and the Cold War

Why are the United States and Israel such strong allies? According to the United States census, Jews compose 2.3 percent of the U.S. population. In the United States, Jews have formed political groups that are highly effective at putting pressure on the U.S. government. Groups such as American Israel Public Affairs Committee (AIPAC), United Jewish Communities, and the American Jewish Congress pressure the U.S. government to vote for more financial aid and political support for Israel.

Additionally, from 1945 to 1990, the United States was involved in the Cold War with the former Soviet Union. These two countries were the most powerful in the world because of their strong militaries and vast numbers of nuclear weapons. Their political and economic systems, however, were so different that they were natural enemies.

A direct war between them could have resulted in nuclear destruction of the planet, so these two superpowers fought each other through their allies. In the Middle East, the Soviet Union supported Syria, the enemy of Israel, sending them thousands of tanks, ammunition, airplanes, and military advisers. To Israel, the United States sent the same. In this manner, the United States and Soviet Union struggled for influence in the Middle East and all over the world. In 1983 at the height of the Cold War, an Israeli invasion into Lebanon could have added dangerous sparks to the Cold War.

In 1980, Pierre Gemayel *(left)* unified his Phalange Party with Camille Chamoun's Lebanese Front, ending the violence between the two parties' militias and paving the way for his son Bashir's election as president of Lebanon in 1982.

Israel Invades Lebanon

Nevertheless, Israel was eager to help Lebanon get rid of the PLO. In the late 1970s, Israel developed a relationship with the leader of the Phalange militia, Bashir Gemayel. Gemayel proved to be a ruthless and effective commander. Young people rallied to his side. By 1980, he had united the various factions of Maronite Christians into one militia that became the Lebanese Armed Forces (LAF). Inheriting control of the Phalange Party from his father, Gemayel enlarged his organization and grew close to Israel.

In 1981, Ariel Sharon became defense minister of Israel and began to plan an invasion of Lebanon to clean out the PLO. In November of that year, Gemayel announced his intention to run for president of Lebanon in the summer of 1982 and he needed Israel's help to win. So, Gemayel and Sharon began to build a joint plan for an Israeli invasion. In the plan, the Israel Defense Force (IDF) would invade southern Lebanon to clear out the PLO, and the LAF would take care of the PLO in Beirut. If the joint operation was successful, Gemayel would likely become president of Lebanon at the end of the summer, and Israel would have a good friend to the north.

Ariel Sharon has been accused of allowing the Sabra and Shatila massacres, which took place when he was Israel's minister of defense in 1982.

In May 1982, Sharon met with Secretary of State Alexander Haig of the United States to get approval for the invasion. Haig agreed in principle that the Middle East needed to be rid of groups like the PLO. On May 28, Haig sent a letter to Israel summarizing his talks with Sharon. While Haig was clear that the United States would support an action in Lebanon only if the PLO acted first, the Israelis felt that the PLO had acted enough. They interpreted the letter as an "OK" from the United States to invade.

Israeli troops cross the Kasmieyeh Bridge in Lebanon. The troops are returning to base after coming under fire from an armed group of Shiite Muslims.

On June 6, 1982, Israeli tanks rolled across the border into southern Lebanon. One tank division swept up the west coast toward Tyre and Sidon, where another force had landed by sea. Another division cleared out the central part of southern Lebanon and attacked Beaufort Castle, from which mortar shells had been launched into Israel.

The Palestinian fighters in southern Lebanon received no aid from their Arab allies. Even the Syrian tanks parked in the Bekaa Valley in eastern Lebanon did not move to protect the Palestinians in the south. All those promises of support had been empty talk. The Israeli tank divisions rolled quickly from town to town through southern Lebanon, cleaning out PLO fighters.

Israel Invades Lebanon

To the Israelis, the battles to rid southern Lebanon of the PLO were a success, but Defense Minister Ariel Sharon wanted more. After all, the PLO headquarters was a few short miles away in West Beirut. The tanks were moving, and Sharon kept pushing his tank commanders northward.

Those tanks rolled over PLO positions and destroyed a number of Shiite villages. Until then, the Shiites had remained mostly small farmers in the south. With their homes destroyed, they were forced northward into the slums of southern Beirut, a poor area that became known as the Belt of Misery. Angering the Shiites would prove to be a mistake.

Within a week of the invasion, the IDF had advanced all the way to Beirut and had decimated Syrian missile batteries in the Bekaa Valley. Syria also lost ninety Soviet-built airplanes and hundreds of tanks. To the Syrian commanders, the Israelis sent a message and a map. The message stated that the Israelis had superior weapons and greater numbers. The map showed the route that the Syrian commanders could use to take their troops back to Syria. Syria left, angered and humiliated.

Throughout the summer of 1982, Israel pounded the PLO in West Beirut without success. Defense Minister Sharon had counted on help from the LAF to get rid of the PLO, but the LAF avoided the fight. What Israel had believed to be a joint operation with the LAF had turned into an Israeli war.

President Ronald Reagan triumphantly announces that U.S. Marines are headed to Lebanon in 1982.

HERE COME THE MARINES

CHAPTER

A month after sending his letter to Israel, Alexander Haig was fired. President Ronald Reagan was unhappy with events in Lebanon, and the United States had come under pressure to do something about it.

As the most powerful nation on Earth, the United States has two roles on the world stage. First, it is a nation that must protect its own people and interests. It is also a protector of freedom and democracy around the world. Freedom and democracy are powerful concepts and deeply held American beliefs. The summer of 1982 left more and more Lebanese civilians dead, injured,

The Attack on U.S. Marines in Lebanon on October 23, 1983

and homeless, and the United States government felt compelled to do something about it. The United States joined the United Nations Multinational Force (MNF), which was preparing to evacuate the PLO from Beirut. If the PLO left, maybe Israel would leave as well. And maybe the fighting in Lebanon would calm down.

On August 23, two days before the MNF was scheduled to land in Beirut, Bashir Gemayel was elected president of Lebanon. However, there were widespread accusations of corruption in the parliament that elected him. It is rumored that the speaker of parliament was paid $10 million for his vote. Two members of parliament who refused to vote had their houses burned to the ground.

On August 25, 1982, U.S. Marines landed at Khalde International Airport in Beirut to evacuate the PLO and enforce peace. To the marines, President Reagan delivered a message, "You are tasked to be once again what marines have been for more than two hundred years—peacemakers . . . I expect that you will perform with the traditional esprit and discipline for which the Marine Corps are renowned."

On September 10, the last of the PLO fighters were evacuated from West Beirut. With them went the U.S. Marines. In return for leaving, the PLO leaders believed that the United States would protect the Palestinian civilians left behind in the refugee camps in West Beirut. They were mistaken.

Here Come the Marines

The Assassination of Bashir Gemayel

On September 14, President-elect Gemayel went to deliver a lecture, as he did every Tuesday afternoon, to a group of women in East Beirut. At 4:10 PM, a bomb placed in the apartment above the lecture hall detonated, killing the Maronite Christian leader.

A Lebanese Christian with ties to Syria was arrested for the bombing. But who had organized it? In addition to Syria, Gemayel had many enemies: the PLO in Beirut, the Druze in the mountains, the Shiites in the slums, and perhaps even Israel, which had been angered by his refusal to commit forces to fighting the PLO. The culprit also could have been one of the factions within the Maronites, for Gemayel's fighters had assassinated several rivals.

In a way, it did not matter who did it. The Phalangists wanted blood—any blood—to spill.

A Massacre

On the evening of September 16, the IDF surrounded the Palestinian refugee camps of Sabra and Shatila in West Beirut. The Israeli forces stood guard, as they permitted Phalangist fighters to "search" the camps. Yet every Israeli, Palestinian, and Maronite Christian knew what would happen.

With no PLO fighters left to defend the Palestinians in the camps, the "search" became a massacre. The number of dead Palestinians may have reached 1,500. Bodies were

Yasser Arafat walks through the streets of West Beirut, examining damage done by Israeli bombs. Particularly hard hit were buildings in the Arab University area.

found in piles in alleys and empty lots, suggesting that the Palestinians were rounded up and executed. In his office in Damascus, PLO leader Yasser Arafat could only watch the horrible images on television and cry.

Arafat and many of his Arab allies felt as if they had been tricked, and they placed blame for the massacre on the Israelis and their backer, the United States. In Lebanon, the name of the United States was dirt.

In Washington, D.C., U.S. government officials were appalled at what they heard and saw. They did not understand the level of hatred among the groups in Lebanon and Israel. How could this have happened, President Reagan asked. Another question was placed before President Reagan: Should we send in the marines again?

Here Come the Marines Again

With the death of Bashir Gemayel, control of the Phalange party and the Lebanese presidency passed to his older brother, Amin. However, Amin Gemayel did not have the same political strength as his brother. Many Christian fighters thought he was weak. As fighting between Maronites and Druze intensified in the Chouf Mountains, and as the Phalangists increasingly ignored him, Amin Gemayel could do nothing to solve his problems. He asked the U.S. Marines to return.

While some U.S. officials argued that sending in troops would only make matters worse, others argued that the United States had indeed let down the Palestinians and the deep beliefs of freedom and democracy. On September 29, 1982, the marines landed again in Beirut.

To the Muslims in Lebanon, the return of the marines was seen as an attempt to keep afloat the Christian government of Amin Gemayel and protect Israel. Although the Americans claimed that they had arrived to keep the peace, few people believed them.

At the site of the suicide bombing of the U.S. Marine barracks, a rescue team digs through the rubble for survivors.

Spring and Summer 1983

CHAPTER 5

At the beginning of 1983, the U.S. Marines stationed in Beirut were in a difficult position. America's marines are trained to land and take the high ground on a mission. To take the high ground in Beirut, however, would require crossing through eastern Beirut and into the Chouf Mountains, where the marines would have to battle the Maronite Christians and the Druze. Back home, the United States government had promised America that its soldiers would not be dying in Beirut. As White House spokesman Larry Speakes had said when the marines first landed, "It is our expectation that

The Attack on U.S. Marines in Lebanon on October 23, 1983

our people will not become involved in any combat that will result in loss of life." How wrong he proved to be.

The marines were stuck at the airport and, worse still, could not return fire. As international peacekeepers, they had been forbidden from firing back unless they were sure of the attacker. Shells, missiles, and bullets were coming from everywhere in greater Beirut. Who was firing each one? No one was sure.

Politically, the United States was in a difficult position, too. The two roles of the United States on the world stage—the most powerful nation and the peacekeeping cop—became confused in Lebanon.

When Amin Gemayel pleaded with the United States to resend the marines, the militias in opposition to Gemayel's Maronite government became suspicious. After the massacres at Sabra and Shatila, no Maronite Christian was punished. In returning to Lebanon, the United States—the peacekeeper—was recognizing the right of the Maronite Christians to rule Lebanon. Was the United States choosing sides when it was supposed to be the peacekeeper?

On February 2, 1983, three Israeli tanks attempted to roll through the area next to Khalde Airport. Marine Captain Charles Johnson climbed onto one of the tanks with his pistol and threatened to shoot if the tank commanders did not pull back. After a dangerous standoff, the Israelis left, convinced that the United States was helping the PLO.

This blindfolded U.S. hostage is paraded in front of the cameras during the 1979 hostage crisis in Iran.

By March of 1983, the United States had no allies in Lebanon, except for the unstable Phalangist government. While U.S. government leaders still believed in their mission, the marines on the ground at Khalde Airport were beginning to lose faith in their ability to make a difference. Their enemies would soon convince them.

U.S. Embassy Attack

In 1979, Islamic students stormed the U.S. Embassy in Tehran, Iran. They captured and held American hostages for 444 days. By the time that the hostages were released, the government of Iran, which had been loyal to the United

The Attack on U.S. Marines in Lebanon on October 23, 1983

States, had been overthrown. A small group of dedicated students had inspired a nation to overthrow a hated government and had humiliated the most powerful nation on Earth.

Inspired by those students, Shiites in Egypt founded a terrorist group in 1979 called Islamic Jihad, which was dedicated to removing the United States and Israel from the holy lands of the Middle East. In the late 1970s, Shiite clerics founded Amal to overthrow the Christian government in Lebanon and gained early support from Iran. In 1982, some Shiites formed a more militant group, Hezbollah, in the southern Beirut slums. These groups became rivals with the same general goals. In the spring of 1983, they were ready to act.

On April 18, 1983, a young man in a leather jacket drove a truck up the driveway of the U.S. Embassy in West Beirut. Approaching the Lebanese guards, he gunned the engine, broke through the barricades, and crashed into the building's entrance, detonating one ton of TNT. The seven-story building collapsed, and sixty-three were killed.

Since the students' takeover of the embassy in Tehran in 1979, security at American embassies had focused on stopping a charging mob. While a supply of tear gas was always near the front gate, defense against a truck storming the gate was weak. As Undersecretary of State Lawrence Engleberger said after the bombing, such an attack "was virtually impossible to defend against if the driver was prepared to commit suicide."

Islamic Jihad claimed responsibility for the attack. An anonymous caller to the offices of *Al-Liwa*, a Middle Eastern newspaper, said, "We shall keep striking at any imperialist presence in Lebanon, including the Multinational Force." In time, the CIA was able to trace responsibility for the attack to Islamic Jihad, sponsored by Iran.

A Bad Treaty

As Ronald Reagan's secretary of state, George Schultz sponsored the 1983 Lebanon-Israel Agreement.

Immediately after the attack, U.S. Secretary of State George Schultz became involved in the peace process. Because of Syria's possible involvement in the bombing at the U.S. Embassy, Schultz spent only nine hours with the Syrians before closing discussions with them. The United States, the nation burying its dead, could not allow Syria to participate in negotiations led by the United States, the peacekeeper.

Nevertheless, on May 17, 1983, Schultz announced the Lebanon-Israel Agreement. Israel agreed to pull back into southern Lebanon, which it would control, provided the PLO and Syria withdrew from Lebanon. However, neither the PLO nor Syria had agreed to anything.

Lebanese citizens flee from the town of Sidon in southern Lebanon after the Israeli invasion. Israeli tanks patrolled southern Lebanon for many months afterward.

Lebanese Muslims had barely been represented at all. Shortly after the agreement was announced, Walid Joumblatt of the PSP, some Maronite Christians who opposed Gemayel, and other Lebanese leaders started a group called the National Salvation Front to overthrow the Gemayel government. The front was suspicious of this treaty that was negotiated by the United States, for it greatly favored Israel, a U.S. ally.

On May 18, Syria closed its doors to U.S. diplomats. Syrian tanks closed off key areas of the Bekaa Valley and blocked valuable trade routes for the Maronite Christians. The Maronites had an agreement, but it was a bad one.

Spring and Summer 1983

For the rest of the summer, various diplomats tried to soften the terms of the withdrawal treaty with Israel. Israel refused. Meanwhile, Israel kept pressuring the Gemayel government to sign a long-term peace treaty. Knowing that other forces in Lebanon were already opposed to his agreement with Israel, Gemayel refused to sign a full peace treaty.

As the hot summer wore on, tempers continued to rise in Beirut. More artillery rounds and missiles landed inside the airport grounds. Attacks also hit the Israelis, even though they had agreed to withdraw. Israel was waiting for the Gemayel government to agree to a full peace treaty and to get organized to occupy the positions that Israel was leaving. At the end of the summer, the Israelis got tired of waiting.

Israel Pulls Back

On September 4, the IDF moved its tanks and troops out of Beirut and the Chouf Mountains to positions south of the Awali River. Immediately, intense fighting broke out between the Christians and the Druze over the positions that Israel had left. The United States tried to get Israel to slow down its withdrawal so that these positions could be occupied by more peace-minded forces. Israel refused.

As Israel strengthened its positions in southern Lebanon, the Druze overran sixty Maronite villages in the Chouf Mountains that Israel had left. Killings were widespread.

PLO leader Yasser Arafat prays before a tombstone memorializing martyrs killed during a monthlong struggle with Phalangist militia during the summer of 1982.

Maronites were dying, and the Phalangist supporter, Israel, was gone. Gemayel's commander of the Lebanese Armed Forces said that he could control West Beirut or the Chouf Mountains sacred to the Maronites, but not both. The Phalangists were in grave trouble.

The United States Loses Neutrality

Despite the confusing events of 1982 and 1983, the U.S. government continued to believe that its support of the Gemayel government and the LAF was helping to secure peace in Lebanon. This belief was exploited.

Spring and Summer 1983

On September 19, 1983, Druze units backed by the Syrians launched a major attack on the Lebanese Armed Forces position at Souk al-Gharb, a strategic village in the Chouf Mountains. The Lebanese commander, General Tannous, appealed to the U.S. military to come to his assistance against this offensive, or the LAF would be overrun. Without confirming the general's claim, U.S. forces began firing artillery from navy cruisers out at sea. When the dust cleared the following morning, it was learned that only eight LAF fighters had been killed in the fighting at Souk al-Gharb. Tannous had tricked the U.S. military into direct support of the LAF; the United States was no longer a peacekeeper. Although marine colonel Timothy Geraghty, the commanding officer of the U.S. forces, had followed his orders, he knew immediately who would suffer the retaliation: the U.S. Marines at the airport.

Ambulances prepare to take away the dead after the collapse of the marines' headquarters.

THE AFTERMATH

CHAPTER 6

So who was the driver of the truck? Who was this man who smiled as he gave his life and took those of 241 marines?

For the U.S. Marines, it was the worst day of casualties since the battle for Iwo Jima in World War II. Within minutes of the attack, the marines learned that the headquarters of the French forces in the MNF had also been hit by a suicide bomber. Their eight-story headquarters collapsed like a house of cards. Over three hundred lives were lost in the span of minutes.

In the aftermath, no group claimed responsibility. Naturally, the marines wanted to fight back. But against whom? Four weeks later, the

The Attack on U.S. Marines in Lebanon on October 23, 1983

marines in Beirut were relieved by other marines and allowed to go home. On February 27, 1984, President Reagan pulled the remaining marines out of Beirut and turned over control of the airport to the Lebanese Armed Forces.

Leaders in the U.S. government sought to place blame for the failure to protect the sleeping marines. After three months of investigation, the official report blamed Colonel Geraghty, the commanding officer of the marine forces. Although his career was ruined, his soldiers did not blame him.

Who Did It?

The identity of the driver may never be known, but we now have a sense of why he committed a murderous act of terrorism. For all of the good intentions of the peacekeeping Multinational Force, the marines were judged first as Americans by the various factions in Lebanon. Arriving after Israel had already invaded, the marines naturally drew suspicion from the Lebanese.

Every step that the marines took was viewed with suspicion by one side or another. When the United States was tricked into supporting General Tannous of the LAF at Souk al-Gharb, its position as a neutral peacekeeper was lost forever. The marines became just another militia in Lebanon.

Although the driver's identity remains a mystery, the identity of the organizer has become clearer. As Colonel Geraghty noted in a November 1983 interview for the Marines Corps Oral History Collection, "There may have

The Aftermath

WHY TERRORISTS ATTACK

The terrorist is part of a small group that is at war with a larger group or nation. The terrorist may feel that the larger group does not understand or does not share the terrorist's beliefs. For example, at the Munich Olympics in 1972, Palestinian terrorists captured and killed eleven Israeli athletes as an act of war against Israel, which they believed was occupying their country.

The terrorist is motivated by politics, economics, religion, or a combination of all of them. For example, the PLO was created as a reaction to losing political control of Palestine to the Israelis. The Israelis, who are Jews, control lands that are sacred to the religion of Islam in which many Palestinians believe. As Israel prospered, the Palestinians in refugee camps in neighboring countries became poorer and poorer. Politics, economics, and religion have all contributed to the conflict.

The terrorist has few regular weapons. Most terrorist organizations cannot fight a normal war against their enemies. The terrorist act becomes a major attack in the terrorist's war against his enemy. For example, in April 1983, terrorists detonated a truck bomb at the U.S. Embassy in Beirut in an attempt to drive the Americans out of Lebanon.

The terrorist attacks civilians to create terror among them. By creating fear, the terrorist inspires the population to get angry with its government. Sometimes, that anger can change what the government does. Forcing those changes is the goal of the terrorist.

The terrorist believes that he is doing the right thing. Some terrorists are willing to give their lives for their cause. There are many examples of suicide attacks, including those involved in the September 11 attacks on the United States and on the U.S. Marines in Beirut.

Cranes remove heavy pieces of rubble from the marine barracks following the bombing in which 241 U.S. servicemen were killed.

been a fanatic driving that truck, but I promise you there was a cold, hard, political, calculating mind behind the planning and execution of it." U.S. officials now believe that the organization behind the attack was either Amal or Hezbollah.

Both groups of poor Muslims had been ignored by the Phalangist government and had been run over by the IDF during the invasion. They had little money, few weapons, and fewer choices. In the religion of Muslims, the term *jihad* means "holy war." A jihad is fought against the enemies of the religion. Fighters who give their lives in a jihad believe that they go to Heaven. It is no wonder that the driver was smiling.

The Aftermath

To acquire the TNT and compressed gases for the attack and then to smuggle them into Beirut required skills and money that these groups did not have. U.S. officials now believe that the government of either Syria or Iran was the sponsor. In the immediate aftermath of the bombing, intelligence agents reported that a large number of individuals fled the Iranian Embassy in Beirut. Did those fleeing people know the truth?

Lessons Learned

In one sense, there are no new lessons to be learned from this tragedy. Terrorism has been around for centuries wherever groups have felt oppressed. Recently, terrorist groups have gained access to better methods of communication, cheaper weapons of destruction, and more explosive power. In light of the September 11, 2001, attacks on the World Trade Center in New York City and the Pentagon, near Washington, D.C., it is clear that terrorists have the ability and the desire to unleash terrible violence in the name of their beliefs.

On the other hand, powerful nations like the United States must become more aware of the good and bad effects of their military actions in foreign countries. The United States was founded on many great and noble principles. In the U.S. Constitution, the rights of every man, woman, and child are protected. In the United States, people are free to believe whatever they want. Shouldn't those beliefs be true for every person on the planet?

Did you notice that short jump? Wasn't it easy to jump from thinking that what is right for the United States is right for everyone in the world?

Many nations do not share the beliefs of the United States. For example, in the U.S. Constitution, religion and government are separated by law. But the government and the religion of nations such as Iran are intertwined. Sometimes, U.S. leaders forget or fail to respect these differences in ways of life. It is this belief in the superiority of the U.S. way of life that angers so many countries and groups.

However, the presence of U.S. soldiers in a troubled country can inspire feelings of great hope, too. In recent years, U.S. peacekeepers have been able to restore peace to places such as Kosovo and Kuwait. The United States is the most powerful nation on Earth. With its enormous power, the United States can also become the keeper of the peace around the world. Yet it is—and will always be—extremely difficult to master both roles at the same time.

After the attack, the U.S. flag and a Marine Corps flag fly above the gate outside the marines' compound in Beirut.

Lives Never Forgotten

For all the answers that the United States provides in the form of soldiers, it must remember to keep asking questions. The soldiers who survived the attack began to ask important questions. Why are we here? What are we trying to do? Who is bombing us? Why can't we fight back? The answers were painful yet important lessons.

Dust rises as this military transport vehicle pulls out of Beirut. It is filled with U.S. Marines headed for home.

What did the terrorists learn? They learned that they can hit and hurt the United States. What they may not have realized is that they killed individuals with good intentions. Although these young men—some not even out of their teens—had been trained to fight and to kill, they were doing what the United Nations and the United States had assigned them to do. They were trying to keep the peace. In standing between the warring militias of Lebanon, the marines were punched hard and knocked down. Bloodied yet determined, they have nevertheless stood again in troubled places all over the world.

GLOSSARY

diaspora A spreading of people out of their country and into the rest of the world.

faction A smaller group within a political group, created when a group of people disagrees with the beliefs or goals of the larger group.

jihad Arabic for "holy war." To Muslims, a jihad is a war against the enemies of the religion.

militia The military of a political party, faction, or area of a country that is not recognized as the armed forces of the country.

Palestine This area located on the east coast of the Mediterranean Sea is controlled by Israel, which was founded in 1948. It is the birthplace of Judaism and Christianity and is sacred to Islam, as well.

sniper A terrorist who hides behind things or on the roofs of buildings and uses a rifle to shoot enemies who cannot see him or her.

suicide attack When a terrorist sacrifices his or her life carrying or driving a bomb into an area, room, or building.

For More Information

American Israel Public Affairs Committee
440 First Street NW #600
Washington, DC 20001
(202) 639-5200
Web site: http://www.aipac.org

American Jewish Congress
15 East Eighty-Fourth Street
New York, NY 10028
(212) 879-4500
Web site: http://ajcongress.org

American Muslim Council
1212 New York Avenue NW
Suite 400
Washington, DC 20005
(202) 789-2262
Web site: http://www.amconline.org

The Attack on U.S. Marines in Lebanon on October 23, 1983

Arab American Institute
1600 K Street NW, Suite 601
Washington, DC 20006
(202) 429-9210
Web site: http://www.aaiusa.org

Embassy of Israel to the United States
3514 International Drive NW
Washington, DC 20008
(202) 364-5500
Web site: http://www.israelemb.org

Lebanon Embassy to the United States
2560 Twenty-Eighth Street NW
Washington, DC 20008
(202) 939-6300
Web site: http://www.lebanonembassyus.org

Web Sites

Due to the changing nature of Internet links, the Rosen Publishing Group, Inc., has developed an online list of Web sites related to the subject of this book. This site is updated regularly. Please use this link to access the list:

http://www.rosenlinks.com/ta/ausm/

For Further Reading

Gaines, Anne. *Terrorism.* Broomall, PA: Chelsea House Publishers, 1998.

Gay, Kathlyn. *Silent Death: The Threat of Chemical and Biological Terrorism.* New York: Twenty-First Century Books, 2001.

Harris, Jonathan. *New Terrorism: Politics of Violence.* Englewood Cliffs, NJ: Silver Burdett Press, 1983.

Landau, Elaine. *Osama bin Laden: A War Against the West.* New York: Twenty-First Century Books, 2002.

Sadler, Amy E., and Paul Winters, eds. *Urban Terrorism.* San Diego: Greenhaven Press, 1996.

BIBLIOGRAPHY

Friedman, Thomas. *From Beirut to Jerusalem.* New York: W.W. Norton & Company, 1988.

Morris, Edmund. *Dutch.* New York: Random House, 1999.

Petit, Michael. *Peacekeepers at War: A Marine's Account of the Beirut Catastrophe.* Boston: Faber and Faber, Inc., 1986.

Pintak, Larry. *Beirut Attacks.* Lexington, MA: Lexington Books, 1982.

Reed, Eli, and Fouad Ajami. *Beirut: City of Regret.* New York: W.W. Norton & Company, 1988.

Schiff, Ze'ev, and Ehud Ya'ari. *Israel's Lebanon War.* Ina Friedman, trans. New York: Simon & Schuster, 1984.

INDEX

A
Arafat, Yasser, 21, 24, 38

B
Beirut, 10, 22, 28, 33, 36, 41, 55
    airport in, 4, 5, 6, 42, 43, 49
    bombing of U.S. Embassy in, 44, 53
    and civil war, 4, 15, 17, 24–25
    culture of, 14
    geography of, 4
    as trade capital, 12, 14

C
Chouf Mountains, 4, 10, 12, 41, 47, 48
Christians, 11–12, 14

D
Druze, 10–11, 12, 13–14, 22, 24, 25, 27, 39, 47, 49

F
France, 11, 12–13, 25

G
Gemayel, Bashir, 30, 31, 36, 39, 42, 46, 47
    assassination of, 37
Green Line, the, 14–15

H
Haig, Alexander, 31, 35

I
Iran, 43–44, 55, 56
Islam, divisions in, 10
Islamic Jihad, 22, 45

Israel, 9–10
    history of, 17–21
    invasion of Lebanon by, 30–33
    and the PLO, 21
    and the U.S., 20–21, 29
Israel Defense Force (IDF), 31, 37, 47

J
Jews, 10, 14, 17–20, 22–23
    in the U.S., 29

K
Khalde Airport, 4, 5, 6, 42, 43

L
Lebanese Armed Forces (LAF), 30, 31, 33, 48, 49, 52
Lebanon
    Christianity in, 11–12
    civil war in, 9, 10, 12, 14, 15, 24–25, 27–28
    French influence in, 11, 12–13
    geography of, 9
    independence of, 13, 17
    invasion by Israel, 30–33
    Islam in, 10–11
    and the PLO, 24–25

M
Maron, John, 11
Maronites, 11–12, 13, 14, 22, 23, 24, 27, 30, 37, 39, 42, 46
Middle East organizations, 22–23
Muslims
    Shiite, 10, 13, 14, 22, 24, 33, 37, 44
    Sunni, 10, 13, 14, 22, 24

The Attack on U.S. Marines in Lebanon on October 23, 1983

N
National Pact, the, 13
Nazis, 20

P
Palestine, 10, 17
    Arabs in, 19–21
    and the British, 19–20
Palestine Liberation Organization (PLO), 21, 23, 24–25, 27–28, 30–33, 36, 37–38, 45, 53
Phalangists, 23, 24, 25, 27, 28, 30, 48, 54
Progressive Socialist Party (PSP), 14

R
Reagan, Ronald, 35, 36, 38–39, 52

S
Schultz, George, 45

September 11, 2001, terrorist attacks, 53, 55
Sharon, Ariel, 31, 33
Soviet Union, 29
Syria, 28, 29, 32, 33, 37, 45, 55

T
terrorism, 52, 53, 55

U
United States Marines
    attack on, 6–7, 51–52
    in Lebanon, 36, 39, 41–42, 49

W
World War I, 19
World War II, 12–13, 20, 51

Z
Zionism, 19, 20, 22

About the Author
Steven P. Olson is a freelance writer who lives in Oakland, California, and likes to travel the world. For more information, visit http://www.stevenolson.com.

Photo Credits
Cover, pp. 5, 16–17, 24, 38, 40–41, 48, 50–51, 54, 56 © AP/Wide World Photos; pp. 8–9 © Samer Mohdad/Corbis; pp. 11, 31, 32, 46, 57 © Judah Passow/Hulton/Archive by Getty Images; p. 13 © Hanan Isachar/Corbis; pp. 15, 18, 25, 43 © Hulton/Archive by Getty Images; pp. 26–27, 30 © Francoise de Mulder/Corbis; pp. 34–35, 45 © Bettmann/Corbis.

Editor
Christine Poolos

Series Design and Layout
Geri Giordano

www.ingramcontent.com/pod-product-compliance
Lightning Source LLC
Chambersburg PA
CBHW041114070526
44584CB00002B/172